T0112611

Additional material copyright © 2015 by Skyhorse Publishing, Inc.

No claim is made to material contained in this work that is derived from government documents. Nevertheless, Skyhorse Publishing claims copyright in all additional content, including, but not limited to, compilation copyright and the copyright in and to any additional material, elements, design, images, or layout of whatever kind included herein.

All inquiries should be addressed to Skyhorse Publishing, 307 West 36th Street, 11th Floor, New York, NY 10018.

Skyhorse Publishing books may be purchased in bulk at special discounts for sales promotion, corporate gifts, fund-raising, or educational purposes. Special editions can also be created to specifications. For details, contact the Special Sales Department, Skyhorse Publishing, 307 West 36th Street, 11th Floor, New York, NY 10018 or info@skyhorsepublishing.com.

Skyhorse® and Skyhorse Publishing® are registered trademarks of Skyhorse Publishing, Inc.®, a Delaware corporation.

Visit our website at www.skyhorsepublishing.com.

10 9 8 7 6 5 4

Library of Congress Cataloging-in-Publication Data is available on file.

Print ISBN: 978-1-62914-478-8
Ebook ISBN: 978-1-63220-180-5

Printed in the United States of America

CONTENTS

SECTION ONE:
THE REVOLUTIONARY YEARS

ACCEPTANCE OF APPOINTMENT, JUNE 15, 1775

Mr. President,

Though I am truly sensible of the high honor done me in this appointment, yet I feel great distress from a consciousness that my abilities and military experience may not be equal to the extensive and important trust. However, as the Congress desire it, I will enter upon the momentous duty and exert every power I possess in the service and for support of the glorious cause. I beg they will accept my most cordial thanks for this distinguished testimony of their approbation. But lest some unlucky event should happen unfavourable to my reputation, I beg it may be remembered by every gentleman in the room, that I this day declare with the utmost sincerity I do not think myself equal to the command I am honored with.

As to pay, Sir, I beg leave to assure the Congress, that as no pecuniary consideration could have tempted me to accept this arduous employment at the expense of my domestic ease and happiness, I do not wish to make any profit from it. I will keep an exact account of my expenses. Those I doubt not they will discharge, and that is all I desire.

LETTER TO GOVERNOR TRUMBULL, JULY 18, 1775

To Governor Trumbull.
Cambridge,
18 July, 1775

Sir,

It is with no small concern, that I find the arrangement of general officers, made by the honorable Continental Congress, has produced much dissatisfaction. As the army is upon a general establishment, their right, to supersede and control a Provincial one, must be unquestionable; and, in such a cause, I should hope every post would be deemed honorable, which gave a man opportunity to serve his country.

A representation from the Congress of this province, with such remarks as occurred to me on this subject, is now before the Continental Congress. In the mean time, I beg leave to assure you, that, unbiassed by any private attachments, I shall studiously endeavor to reconcile their pretensions to their duty, and so dispose them, as to prevent, as far as possible, any inconvenience to the public service from this competition.

I have the honor to be,
&c.

LETTER TO JOSEPH REED, JANUARY 14, 1776

To Joseph Reed.
Cambridge,
14 January, 1776

Dear Sir,
The bearer presents an opportunity to me of acknowledging the receipt of your favor of the 30th ultimo, (which never came to my hands till last night), and, if I have not done it before, of your other of the 23d preceding.

The hints you have communicated from time to time not only deserve, but do most sincerely and cordially meet with my thanks. You cannot render a more acceptable service, nor in my estimation give a more convincing proof of your friendship, than by a free, open, and undisguised account of every matter relative to myself or conduct. I can bear to hear of imputed or real errors. The man, who wishes to stand well in the opinion of others, must do this; because he is thereby enabled to correct his faults, or remove prejudices which are imbibed against him. For this reason, I shall thank you for giving me the opinions of the world, upon such points as you know me to be interested in; for, as I have but one capital object in view, I could wish to make my conduct coincide with the wishes of mankind, as far as I can consistently; I mean, without departing from that great line of duty, which, though hid under a cloud for some time, from a peculiarity of circumstances, may nevertheless bear a scrutiny. My constant attention to the great and perplexing objects, which continually rise to my view, absorbs all lesser considerations, and indeed scarcely allows me time to reflect, that there is such a body in existence as the General Court of this colony, but when I am reminded of it by a committee; nor can I, upon recollection, discover in what instances (I wish they would be more explicit) I have been inattentive to, or slighted them. They could not, surely, conceive that there was a propriety in unbosoming the secrets of an army to them; that it was necessary to ask their opinion of throwing up an intrenchment, forming a battalion, &c., &c. It must, therefore, be what I before hinted to you; and how to remedy it I hardly know, as I am acquainted with few of the members, never go out of my own lines, or see any of them in them.

I am exceeding sorry to hear, that your little fleet has been shut in by the frost. I hope it has sailed ere this, and given you some proof of the utility of it, and enabled the Congress to bestow a little more attention to the affairs of this army, which suffers exceedingly by their overmuch business, or too little attention to it. We are now without any money in our treasury, powder in our magazines, arms in our stores. We are without a brigadier (the want of which has been twenty times urged), engineers, expresses (though a committee has been appointed these two months to establish them), and by and by, when we shall be called upon to take the field, shall not have a tent to lie in. Apropos, what is doing with mine?

These are evils, but small in comparison of those, which disturb my present repose. Our enlistments are at a stand; the fears I ever entertained are realized; that is, the discontented officers (for I do not know how else to account for it) have thrown such difficulties or stumbling-blocks in the way of recruiting, that I no longer entertain a hope of completing the army by voluntary enlistments, and I see no move or likelihood of one, to do it by other means. In the last two weeks we have enlisted but about a thousand men; whereas I was confidently bid to believe, by all the officers I conversed with, that we should by this time have had the regiments nearly completed. Our total number upon paper amounts to about ten thousand five hundred; but as a large portion of these are returned not joined, I never expect to receive them, as an ineffectual order has once issued to call them in. Another is now gone forth, peremptorily requiring all officers under pain of being cashiered, and recruits as being treated as deserters, to join their respective regiments by the 1st day of next month, that I may know my real strength; but if my fears are not imaginary, I shall have a dreadful account of the advanced month's pay. In consequence of the assurances given, and my expectation of having at least men enough enlisted to defend our lines, to which may be added my unwillingness of burthening the cause with unnecessary expense, no relief of militia has been ordered in, to supply the places of those, who are released from their engagements to-morrow, and on whom, though many have promised to continue out the month, there is no security for their stay.

Thus am I situated with respect to men. With regard to arms I am yet worse off. Before the dissolution of the old army, I issued an order directing three judicious men of each brigade to attend, review, and appraise the good arms of every regiment; and finding a very great unwillingness in the men to part with their arms, at the same time not having it in my power to pay them for the months of November and December, I threatened severely, that every soldier, who carried away his firelock without leave, should never receive pay for those months;

yet so many have been carried off, partly by stealth, but chiefly as condemned, that we have not at this time one hundred guns in the stores, of all that have been taken in the prize-ship and from the soldiery, notwithstanding our regiments are not half complete. At the same time I am told, and believe it, that to restrain the enlistment to men with arms, you will get but few of the former, and still fewer of the latter, which would be good for any thing.

How to get furnished I know not. I have applied to this and the neighboring colonies, but with what success time only can tell. The reflection on my situation, and that of this army, produces many an uneasy hour when all around me are wrapped in sleep. Few people know the predicament we are in, on a thousand accounts; fewer still will believe, if any disaster happens to these lines, from what causes it flows. I have often thought how much happier I should have been, if, instead of accepting of a command under such circumstances, I had taken my musket on my shoulder and entered the ranks, or, if I could have justified the measure to posterity and my own conscience, had retired to the back country, and lived in a wigwam. If I shall be able to rise superior to these and many other difficulties, which might be enumerated, I shall most religiously believe, that the finger of Providence is in it, to blind the eyes of our enemies; for surely if we get well through this month, it must be for want of their knowing the disadvantages we labor under.

Could I have foreseen the difficulties, which have come upon us; could I have known, that such a backwardness would have been discovered in the old soldiers to the service, all the generals upon earth should not have convinced me of the propriety of delaying an attack upon Boston till this time. When it can now be attempted, I will not undertake to say; but thus much I will answer for, that no opportunity can present itself earlier than my wishes. But as this letter discloses some interesting truths, I shall be somewhat uneasy until I hear it gets to your hands, although the conveyance is thought safe.

We made a successful attempt a few nights ago upon the houses near Bunker's Hill. A party under Major Knowlton crossed upon the mill-dam, the night being dark, and set fire to and burnt down eight out of fourteen which were standing, and which we found they were daily pulling down for fuel. Five soldiers, and the wife of one of them, inhabiting one of the houses, were brought off prisoners; another soldier was killed; none of ours hurt.

Having undoubted information of the embarkation of troops, somewhere from three to five hundred, at Boston, and being convinced they are designed either for New York government (from whence we have some very disagreeable accounts of the conduct of the Tories) or Virginia, I despatched General Lee a few days ago, in order to secure the city of New York from falling into their hands, as the consequences of such a blow might prove fatal to our interests. He is also to inquire a little into the conduct of the Long-Islanders, and such others as have, by their conduct and declarations, proved themselves inimical to the common cause.

To effect these purposes, he is to raise volunteers in Connecticut, and call upon the troops of New Jersey, if not contrary to any order of Congress.

By a ship just arrived at Portsmouth, New Hampshire, we have London prints to the 2d of November, containing the addresses of Parliament, which contain little more than a repetition of the speech, with assurances of standing by his Majesty with lives and fortunes. The captains (for there were three or four of them passengers) say, that we have nothing to expect but the most vigorous exertions of administration, who have a dead majority upon all questions, although the Duke of Grafton and General Conway have joined the minority, as also the Bishop of Peterborough. These captains affirm confidently, that the five regiments from Ireland cannot any of them have arrived at Halifax, inasmuch as that by a violent storm on the 19th of October, the transports were forced, in a very distressful condition, into Milford Haven (Wales) and were not in a condition to put to sea when they left London, and the weather has been such since, as to prevent heavy loaded ships from making a passage by this time. One or two transports, they add, were thought to be lost; but these arrived some considerable time ago at Boston, with three companies of the 17th regiment.

Mr. Sayre has been committed to the Tower, upon the information of a certain Lieutenant or Adjutant Richardson (formerly of your city) for treasonable practices; an intention of seizing his Majesty, and possessing himself of the Tower, it is said in "The Crisis." But he is admitted to bail himself in five hundred pounds, and two sureties in two hundred and fifty pounds each.

What are the conjectures of the wise ones with you, of the French armament in the West Indies? But previous to this, is there any certainty of such an armament? The captains, who are sensible men, heard nothing of this when they left England; nor does there appear any apprehensions on this score in any of the measures or speeches of administration. I should think the Congress will not, ought not, to adjourn at this important crisis. But it is highly necessary, when I am at the end of a second sheet of paper, that I should adjourn my account of matters to another letter. I shall, therefore, in Mrs. Washington's name, thank you for your good wishes towards her, and with her compliments, added to mine, to Mrs. Reed, conclude,

dear Sir,
your sincere and affectionate servant.

LETTER TO JOSIAH QUINCY, MARCH 24, 1776

Cambridge 24th March 1776.

Sir,
I am favour'd with your Letter of the 21st Instt. —
it came to hand this afternoon, and I thank you
for the many polite and flattering expressions
which it contains. To obtain the applause of
deserving men, is a heart felt satisfaction — to
merit them, is my highest wish. If my conduct
therefore [strikeout] as an Instrument in the
late signal interposition of Providence hath
merited the approbation of the great Country,
I shall esteem it one of the most fortunate &
happy events of my life. I acknowledge myself
yr debtor, for the share you have bestowed on
me of it.

The continuance of the Fleet in Nantasket
Road affords matter for speculation – it
surpasses my comprehension and awakens all my
suspicions. I have taken every step in my power
to guard against surprizes, but the temper of
your People seems to me to be, to apprehend no
danger till it stares them in Face. I do not think
there is cause to apprehend such Marauding
parties as you dread – if any stroke is aimed,
it will be a capitol one, for which reason I wish
to be much upon my guard; & therefore have
appointed Guard Boats, lookouts &ca. There is
one evil I dread, & that is their Spies, I could
wish therefore that the most attentive watch
was kept to prevent any Intercourse between
the ship & main – for this purpose, and to
prevent suspected persons (for I have no doubt
but that trusty soldiers, Sergeants, and even
commissioned officers in disguise will be sent
out) from travelling about, I wish a dozen or
more of Honest, sensible, and deligent Men were
employed to haunt the Communication between
Roxbury, and the different landing Places
nearest the Shipping, in order to question; cross

question &ca all such Persons as are unknown, & cannot give an acct. of themselves in a strait, & satisfactory line. If you could hire Men for this purpose whilst the shipping continue where they now are, I would pay the wages you shall agree upon; and thank you for the trouble, as I think it a matter of some Importance to prevent them from obtaining Intelligence of our Situation. The earliest Information should also be communicated of any movements which may be discovered, and whether any of the shipping are getting out, as it were by stealth.

I am exceedingly sorry to hear of your Indisposition, & heartily wish you a perfect restoration of health. I should be very happy to take you by the hand before I bid adieu to the Colony, but as my motions are regulated by those of the Enemy, I cannot say how – when – or where it can happen.

In sincerity and truth I remain
Dr Sir Yr most Obedt & Obligd Servt
Go: Washington

TO THE PRESIDENT OF CONGRESS, SEPTEMBER 24, 1776

Colo. Morris's, on the Heights of Haerlem,
24 September, 1776

Sir,
From the hours allotted to sleep, I will borrow a few moments to convey my thoughts on sundry important matters to Congress. I shall offer them with the sincerity, which ought to characterize a man of candor, and with the freedom, which may be used in giving useful information without incurring the imputation of presumption.

We are now, as it were, upon the eve of another dissolution of our army. The remembrance of the difficulties, which happened upon that occasion last year, and the consequences, which might have followed the change if proper advantages had been taken by the enemy, added to a knowledge of the present temper and situation of the troops, reflect but a very gloomy prospect in the appearances of things now, and satisfy me beyond the possibility of doubt, that, unless some speedy and effectual measures are adopted by Congress, our cause will be lost. It is in vain to expect, that any more than a trifling part of this army will again engage in the service on the encouragement offered by Congress. When men find that their townsmen and companions are receiving twenty, thirty, and more dollars for a few months' service, which is truly the case, it cannot be expected, without using compulsion; and to force them into the service would answer no valuable purpose. When men are irritated, and their passions inflamed, they fly hastily and cheerfully to arms; but, after the first emotions are over, to expect among such people as compose the bulk of an army, that they are influenced by any other principles than those of interest, is to look for what never did, and I fear never will happen; the Congress will deceive themselves, therefore, if they expect it. A soldier, reasoned with upon the goodness of the cause he is engaged in, and the inestimable rights he is contending for, hears you with patience, and acknowledges the truth of your observations, but adds that it is of no more importance to him than to others. The officer makes you the same reply, with this further remark, that his pay will not support him, and he cannot ruin himself and family to serve his country, when every member of the community is equally interested, and benefitted by his labors. The few, therefore, who act upon principles of disinterestedness, comparatively speaking, are no more than a drop in the ocean.

It becomes evident to me then, that, as this contest is not likely to be the work of a day, as the war must be carried on systematically, and to do it you must have good officers, there are in my judgment no other possible means to obtain them but by establishing your army upon a permanent footing, and giving your officers good pay. This will induce gentlemen and men of character to engage; and, till the bulk of your officers is composed of such persons as are actuated by principles of honor and a spirit of enterprise, you have little to expect from them. They ought to have such allowances, as will enable them to live like and support the character of gentlemen, and not be driven by a scanty pittance to the low and dirty arts, which many of them practise, to filch from the public more than the difference of pay would amount to, upon an ample allowance. Besides, something is due to the man, who puts his life in your hands, hazards his health, and forsakes the sweets of domestic enjoyment. Why a captain in the Continental service should receive no more than five shillings currency per day for performing the same duties, that an officer of the same rank in the British service receives ten shillings for, I never could conceive; especially when the latter is provided with every necessary he requires upon the best terms, and the former can scarce procure them at any rate. There is nothing that gives a man consequence and renders him fit for command, like a support that renders him independent of every body but the state he serves.

With respect to the men, nothing but a good bounty can obtain them upon a permanent establishment; and for no shorter time, than the continuance of the war, ought they to be engaged; as facts incontestably prove, that the difficulty and cost of enlistments increase with time. When the army was first raised at Cambridge, I am persuaded the men might have been got, without a bounty, for the war. After this, they began to see that the contest was not likely to end so speedily as was imagined, and to feel their consequence by remarking, that, to get in their militia in the course of the last year, many towns were induced to give them a bounty. Foreseeing the evils resulting from this, and the destructive consequences, which unavoidably would follow short enlistments, I took the liberty in a long letter written by myself to recommend the enlistments for and during the war, assigning such reasons for it as experience has since convinced me were well founded. At that time, twenty dollars would, I am persuaded, have engaged the men for this term. But it will not do to look back; and, if the present opportunity is slipped, I am persuaded that twelve months more will increase our difficulties fourfold. I shall therefore take the freedom of giving it as my opinion, that a good bounty should be immediately offered, aided by the proffer of at least a hundred or a hundred and fifty acres of land, and a suit of clothes and blanket to each non-comissioned officer and soldier; as I have good authority for saying, that, however high the men's pay may appear, it is barely sufficient, in the present scarcity and dearness of all kinds of goods, to keep them in clothes, much less afford support to their families.

If this encouragement then is given to the men, and such pay allowed the officers as will induce gentlemen of character and liberal sentiments to engage, and proper care and precaution are used in the nomination, (having more regard to the characters of persons, than to the number of men they can enlist), we should in a little time have an army able to cope with any that can be opposed to it, as there are excellent materials to form one out of. But while the only merit an officer possesses is his ability to raise men, while those men consider and treat him as an equal, and, in the character of an officer, regard him no more than a broomstick, being mixed together as one common herd, no order nor discipline can prevail; nor will the officer ever meet with that respect, which is essentially necessary to due subordination.

To place any dependence upon militia is assuredly resting upon a broken staff. Men just dragged from the tender scenes of domestic life, unaccustomed to the din of arms, totally unacquainted with every kind of military skill, (which being followed by want of confidence in themselves, when opposed to troops regularly trained, disciplined, and appointed, superior in knowledge and superior in arms,) makes them timid and ready to fly from their own shadows. Besides the sudden change in their manner of living, (particularly in the lodging,) brings on sickness in many, impatience in all, and such an unconquerable desire of returning to their respective homes, that it not only produces shameful and scandalous desertions among themselves, but infuses the like spirit in others.

Again, men accustomed to unbounded freedom and no control cannot brooke the restraint, which is indispensably necessary to the good order and government of an army; without which, licentiousness and every kind of disorder triumphantly reign. To bring men to a proper degree of subordination is not the work of a day, a month, or even a year; and, unhappily for us and the cause we are engaged in, the little discipline I have been laboring to establish in the army under my immediate command is in a manner done away, by having such a mixture of troops, as have been called together within these few months.

Relaxed and as unfit as our rules and regulations of war are for the government of an army, the militia (those properly so called, for of these we have two sorts, the six-months' men, and those sent in as a temporary aid) do not think themselves subject to them, and therefore take liberties, which the soldier is punished for. This creates jealousy; jealousy begets dissatisfaction; and these by degrees ripen into mutiny, keeping the whole army in a confused and disordered state, rendering the time of those, who wish to see regularity and good order prevail, more unhappy than words can describe. Besides this, such repeated changes take place, that all arrangement is set at nought, and the constant fluctuation of things deranges every plan as fast as adopted.

These, Sir, Congress may be assured, are but a small part of the inconveniences, which might be enumerated, and attributed to militia; but there is one, that merits particular attention, and that is the expense. Certain I am, that it would be cheaper to keep fifty or a hundred thousand in constant pay, than to depend upon half the number and supply the other half occasionally by militia. The time the latter are in pay before and after they are in camp, assembling and marching, the waste of ammunition, the consumption of stores, which, in spite of every resolution or requisition of Congress, they must be furnished with, or sent home, added to other incidental expenses consequent upon their coming and conduct in camp, surpasses all idea, and destroys every kind of regularity and economy, which you could establish among fixed and settled troops, and will, in my opinion, prove, if the scheme is adhered to, the ruin of our cause.

The jealousy of a standing army, and the evils to be apprehended from one, are remote, and, in my judgment, situated and circumstanced as we are, not at all to be dreaded; but the consequence of wanting one, according to my ideas formed from the present view of things, is certain and inevitable ruin. For, if I was called upon to declare upon oath, whether the militia have been most serviceable or hurtful upon the whole, I should subscribe to the latter. I do not mean by this, however, to arraign the conduct of Congress; in so doing I should equally condemn my own measures, if I did not my judgment; but experience, which is the best criterion to work by, so fully, clearly, and decisively reprobates the practice of trusting to militia, that no man, who regards order, regularity, and economy, or who has any regard for his own honor, character, or peace of mind, will risk them upon this issue.

No less attention should be paid to the choice of surgeons, than of other officers of the army. They should undergo a regular examination, and, if not appointed by the director-general and surgeons of the hospital, they ought to be subordiate to and governed by his directions. The regimental surgeons I am speaking of, many of whom are very great rascals, countenancing the men in sham complaints to exempt them from duty, and often receiving bribes to certify indispositions, with a view to procure discharges or furloughs; but, independent of these practices, while they are considered as unconnected with the general hospital, there will be nothing but continual complaints of each other; the director of the hospital charging them with enormity in their drafts for the sick, and they him with the same for denying such things as are necessary. In short, there is a constant bickering among them, which tends greatly to the injury of the sick, and will always subsist till the regimental surgeons are made to look up to the director-general of the hospital as a superior. Whether this is the case in regular armies or not, I cannot undertake to say; but certain I am, there is a necessity for it in this, or the sick will suffer. The regimental surgeons are aiming, I am persuaded, to break up the general hospital, and have, in numberless instances, drawn for medicines and stores in the most profuse and extravagant manner for private purposes.

Another matter highly worthy of attention is, that other rules and regulations may be adopted for the government of the army, than those now in existence; otherwise the army, but for the name, might as well be disbanded. For the most atrocious offences, one or two instances only excepted, a man receives no more than thirty-nine lashes; and these, perhaps, through the collusion of the officer, who is to see it inflicted, are given in such a manner as to become rather a matter of sport than punishment; but, when inflicted as they ought, many hardened fellows, who have been the subjects, have declared that, for a bottle of rum, they would undergo a second operation. It is evident, therefore, that this punishment is inadequate to many crimes it is assigned to. As a proof of it, thirty or forty soldiers will desert at a time, and of late a practice prevails (as you will see by my letter of the 22d) of the most alarming nature and which will, if it cannot be checked, prove fatal both to the country and army; I mean the infamous practice of plundering. For, under the idea of Tory property, or property that may fall into the hands of the enemy, no man is secure in his effects, and scarcely in his person. In order to get at them, we have several instances of people being frightened out of their houses, under pretence of those houses being ordered to be burnt, and this is done with a view of seizing the goods; nay, in order that the villany may be more effectually concealed, some houses have actually been burnt, to cover the theft. I have, with some others, used my utmost endeavors to stop this horrid practice; but under the present lust after plunder, and want of laws to punish offenders, I might almost as well attempt to remove Mount Atlas. I have ordered instant corporal punishment upon every man, who passes our lines, or is seen with plunder, that the offenders might be punished for disobedience of orders; and enclose to you the proceedings of a court-martial held upon an officer [Ensign Matthew McCumber] who, with a party of men, had robbed a house a little beyond our lines of a number of valuable goods, among which (to show that nothing escapes) were four large pier looking-glasses, women's clothes, and other articles, which, one would think, could be of no earthly use to him. He was met by a major of brigade, [Box] who ordered him to return the goods, as taken contrary to general orders, which he not only peremptorily refused to do, but drew up his party, and swore he would defend them at the hazard of his life; on which I ordered him to be arrested and tried for plundering, disobedience of orders, and mutiny. For the result, I refer to the proceedings of the court, whose judgment appeared so exceedingly extraordinary, that I ordered a reconsideration of the matter, upon which, and with the assistance of a fresh evidence, they made a shift to cashier him. I adduce this instance, to give some idea to Congress of the current sentiments and general run of the officers, which compose the present army; and to show how exceedingly necessary it is to be careful in the choice of the new set, even if it should take double the time to complete the levies.

An army formed of good officers moves like clockwork; but there is no situation upon earth less enviable, nor more distressing, than that person's, who is at the head of troops which are regardless of order and discipline, and who are unprovided with almost every necessary. In a word, the difficulties, which have for ever surrounded me since I have been in the service, and kept my mind constantly upon the stretch, the wounds, which my feelings as an officer have received by a thousand things, which have happened contrary to my expectation and wishes; the effect of my own conduct, and present appearance of things, so little pleasing to myself, as to render it a matter of no surprise to me if I should stand capitally censured by Congress; added to a consciousness of my inability to govern an army composed of such discordant parts, and under such a variety of intricate and perplexing circumstances;—induces not only a belief, but a thorough conviction in my mind, that it will be impossible, unless there is a thorough change in our military system, for me to conduct matters in such a manner as to give satisfaction to the public, which is all the recompense I aim at, or ever wished for.

Before I conclude, I must apologize for the liberties taken in this letter, and for the blots and scratchings therein, not having time to give it more correctly. With truth I can add, that, with every sentiment of respect and esteem, I am yours and the Congress's most obedient, &c.

LETTER TO BRYAN FAIRFAX, SEPTEMBER 25, 1777

Dear Sir,

Despairing of seeing the bearer again, I wrote an answer to your favour from the Conestoga Waggon (without date) yesterday; and put it into the hands of a Man who faithfully promised to deliver it – since w[h]en your own Messenger has called upon me, & that you may have two chances of getting my passport to the Camp, you will receive one under this cover.

In my Letter of yesterday I assur'd you, and assur'd you with truth, that the difference in our political Sentiments had made no change in my friendship for you. I esteem, and revere, every man who acts from principle as I am persuaded you do; and shall ever contribute my aid to facilitate any Inclination you may wish to endulge, as I am satisfied that that honr. which I have ever found you scrupulously observant of, will never be departed from. I shall add no more, because in the first place, I have very little leizure, & on the next, because I conceive it unnecessary to multiply words to prove that with sincere regard

I am Dr Sir
Yr Most Obedt & Affe
Go: Washington

LETTER TO LORD STIRLING, MARCH 5, 1780

To Lord Stirling.
[PRIVATE.]
Morris-town,
5 March, 1780

My Lord,
I have read the orders, which you had framed for your division. They are certainly good; but in substance, except in a very few instances, are very explicitly enjoined by the regulations, and have been reiterated at different periods in the general orders, antecedent to the promulgation of the established "regulations for the Order and Discipline of the Troops," and since in many particular ones by a reference to them; as your Lordship may perceive by recurring to the Orderly Book. At our last interview I slightly

touched on this subject; but I shall embrace the present occasion to repeat more fully, that orders, unless they are followed by close attention to the performance of them, are of little avail. They are read by some, only heard of by others, and inaccurately attended to by all, whilst by a few they are totally disregarded; and this will for ever be the case, till the principal officers of the army begin the work of reformation by a close inspection into the police, the conduct of the officers, and men under their respective commands, and will endeavor to restore public economy and saving, than which nothing can better suit our present circumstances.

Example, whether it be good or bad, has a powerful influence, and the higher in Rank the officer is, who sets it, the more striking it is. Hence, and from all military experience, it has been found necessary for officers of every denomination to inspect narrowly the conduct of such parts of the army and corps, as are committed to their care. Without this, the regulations "for the Order and Discipline of the Troops," established by the highest authority, and which are short, simple, and easy in the performers, and the General orders, will be little attended to; of course neglect of discipline, want of order, irregularity, waste, abuse, and embezzlement of public property, insensibly creep in. It is idle to suppose, under a description like this, ye ground for which none I believe will deny, that a division, Brigade, or Regimental order, will have greater weight than those of Congress, or yr. Xc.; but, if the Persons issuing them would devote, as duty indispensably requires, a reasonable portion of their time to a personal and close inspection into the affairs of their respective commands; would frequently parade their Regiments, and compare the actual strength of them, their arms, accoutrements, and cloathes, with the returns, and have the deficiencies, (if any there be,) satisfactorily accounted for and provided, agreeably to the establishment of the army; would see that the regulations, the general orders, and their own, were carried into execution, where practicable, or report the causes of failure when they cannot; that all returns are made in due form, in proper time, and correctly, comparing one return with another, in order to prevent mistakes, correct abuses, and do justice to the public; and that, in visiting such parts of the line, and such particular corps, as are entrusted to their care, praise is bestowed on the deserving, reprehension, and, (where necessary,) punishment on the negligent; the good effect would be almost instantaneously felt. Frequent visits and inspection into matters of this kind would produce more real good in one month, than volumes of the best digested orders, that the wit of man can devise, wd. accomplish in seven years.

Were it not for the infinity of perplexing business, that is referred to and comes before me from every quarter; the multiplicity of Letters and papers I have to read and consider, many of which originate in the want of application and due attention being given by the Genl. officers to their respective commands, which brings a variety of applications to head-Qrs., that ought to be settled in the respective lines, I should devote much more of my time to the military parts of my duty. Unhappily, while necessity with-holds me from these attentions, a want of being sufficiently impressed with its importance, or some other cause, operates with equal force on others; and the few rides I am able to make to the Camp, and the hours which. I can devote to the business of the line, never fail producing mortifying proofs of inattention and relaxation of discipline. The Country, in all my excursions, I find spread over with soldiers, notwithstanding the pointed orders which have been issued to restrain them, and to discountenance a practice, which. has been found pregnant of desertion, robbery, and even murders, and totally repugnant to every principle of discipline and the Rules laid down for our government.

This, my Lord, is a free and friendly representation of facts. Your letter drew it from *me* to *you* at this time; but I shall take occasion, so soon as the Genl. officers assemble, to require in explicit terms from them a conduct conformable to these sentiments in future; for without it there is no possibility in the present perplexity of affairs, and the divided attention I am obliged to give to the numberless objects, which. press upon me, to move the military machine with any degree of propriety without their assistance. With much esteem and regard, I am your Lordship's, &c.

SPEECH,
MARCH 15, 1783

Gentlemen:

By an anonymous summons, an attempt has been made to convene you together; how inconsistent with the rules of propriety, how unmilitary, and how subversive of all order and discipline, let the good sense of the army decide...

Thus much, gentlemen, I have thought it incumbent on me to observe to you, to show upon what principles I opposed the irregular and hasty meeting which was proposed to have been held on Tuesday last - and not because I wanted a disposition to give you every opportunity consistent with your own honor, and the dignity of the army, to make known your grievances. If my conduct heretofore has not evinced to you that I have been a faithful friend to the army, my declaration of it at this time would be equally unavailing and improper. But as I was among the first who embarked in the cause of our common country. As I have never left your side one moment, but when called from you on public duty. As I have been the constant companion and witness of your distresses, and not among the last to feel and acknowledge your merits. As I have ever considered my own military reputation as inseparably connected with that of the army. As my heart has ever expanded with joy, when I have heard its praises, and my indignation has arisen, when the mouth of detraction has been opened against it, it can scarcely be supposed, at this late stage of the war, that I am indifferent to its interests.

But how are they to be promoted? The way is plain, says the anonymous addresser. If war continues, remove into the unsettled country, there establish yourselves, and leave an ungrateful country to defend itself. But who are they to defend? Our wives, our children, our farms, and other property which we leave behind us. Or, in this state of hostile separation, are we to take the two first (the latter cannot be removed) to perish in a wilderness, with hunger, cold, and nakedness? If peace takes place, never sheathe your swords, says he, until you have obtained full and ample justice; this dreadful alternative, of either deserting our country in the extremest hour of her distress or turning our arms against it (which is the apparent object, unless Congress can be compelled into instant compliance), has something so shocking in it that humanity revolts at the idea. My God! What can this writer have in view, by recommending such measures? Can he be a friend to the army? Can he be a friend to this country? Rather, is he not an insidious foe? Some emissary, perhaps, from New York, plotting the ruin of both, by sowing the seeds of discord and separation between the civil and military powers of the continent? And what a compliment does he pay to our understandings when he recommends measures in either alternative, impracticable in their nature?

I cannot, in justice to my own belief, and what I have great reason to conceive is the intention of Congress, conclude this address, without giving it as my decided opinion, that that honorable body entertain exalted sentiments of the services of the army; and, from a full conviction of its merits and sufferings, will do it complete justice. That their endeavors to discover and establish funds for this purpose have been unwearied, and will not cease till they have succeeded, I have not a doubt. But, like all other large bodies, where there is a variety of different interests to reconcile, their deliberations are slow. Why, then, should we distrust them? And, in consequence of that distrust, adopt measures which may cast a shade over that glory which has been so justly acquired; and tarnish the reputation of an army which is celebrated through all Europe, for its fortitude and patriotism? And for what is this done? To bring the object we seek nearer? No! most certainly, in my opinion, it will cast it at a greater distance.

For myself (and I take no merit in giving the assurance, being induced to it from principles of gratitude, veracity, and justice), a grateful sense of the confidence you have ever placed in me, a recollection of the cheerful assistance and prompt obedience I have experienced from you, under every vicissitude of fortune, and the sincere affection I feel for an army I have so long had the honor to command will oblige me to declare, in this public and solemn manner, that, in the attainment of complete justice for all your toils and dangers, and in the gratification of every wish, so far as may be done consistently with the great duty I owe my country and those powers we are bound to respect, you may freely command my services to the utmost of my abilities.

While I give you these assurances, and pledge myself in the most unequivocal manner to exert whatever ability I am possessed of in your favor, let me entreat you, gentlemen, on your part, not to take any measures which, viewed in the calm light of reason, will lessen the dignity and sully the glory you have hitherto maintained; let me request you to rely on the plighted faith of your country, and place a full confidence in the purity of the intentions of Congress; that, previous to your dissolution as an army, they will cause all your accounts to be fairly liquidated, as directed in their resolutions, which were published to you two days ago, and that they will adopt the most effectual measures in their power to render ample justice to you, for your faithful and meritorious services. And let me conjure you, in the name of our common country, as you value your own sacred honor, as you respect the rights of humanity, and as you regard the military and national character of America, to express your utmost horror and detestation of the man who wishes, under any specious pretenses, to overturn the liberties of our country, and who wickedly attempts to open the floodgates of civil discord and deluge our rising empire in blood.

By thus determining and thus acting, you will pursue the plain and direct road to the attainment of your wishes. You will defeat the insidious designs of our enemies, who are compelled to resort from open force to secret artifice. You will give one more distinguished proof of unexampled patriotism and patient virtue, rising superior to the pressure of the most complicated sufferings. And you will, by the dignity of your conduct, afford occasion for posterity to say, when speaking of the glorious example you have exhibited to mankind, "Had this day been wanting, the world had never seen the last stage of perfection to which human nature is capable of attaining."

General George Washington - March 15, 1783

LETTER TO THE GOVERNORS OF ALL THE STATES (ON DISBANDING THE ARMY), JUNE 8, 1783

CIRCULAR LETTER ADDRESSED TO THE GOVERNORS OF ALL THE STATES ON DISBANDING THE ARMY.

Head-Quarters,
Newburg,
8 June, 1783

Sir,

The great object, for which I had the honor to hold an appointment in the service of my country, being accomplished, I am now preparing to resign it into the hands of Congress, and to return to that domestic retirement, which, it is well known, I left with the greatest reluctance; a retirement for which I have never ceased to sigh, through a long and painful absence, and in which (remote from the noise and trouble of the world) I meditate to pass the remainder of life, in a state of undisturbed repose. But before I carry this resolution into effect, I think it a duty incumbent on me to make this my last official communication; to congratulate you on the glorious events which Heaven has been pleased to produce in our favor; to offer my sentiments respecting some important subjects, which appear to me to be intimately connected with the tranquillity of the United States; to take my leave of your Excellency as a public character; and to give my final blessing to that country, in whose service I have spent the prime of my life, for whose sake I have consumed so many anxious days and watchful nights, and whose happiness, being extremely dear to me, will always constitute no inconsiderable part of my own.

Impressed with the liveliest sensibility on this pleasing occasion, I will claim the indulgence of dilating the more copiously on the subjects of our mutual felicitation. When we consider the magnitude of the prize we contended for, the doubtful nature of the contest, and the favorable manner in which it has terminated, we shall find the greatest possible reason for gratitude and rejoicing. This is a theme that will afford infinite delight to every benevolent and liberal mind, whether the event in contemplation be considered as the source of present enjoyment, or the parent of future happiness; and we shall have equal occasion to felicitate ourselves on the lot which Providence has assigned us, whether we view it in a natural, a political, or moral point of light.

The citizens of America, placed in the most enviable condition, as the sole lords and proprietors of a vast tract of continent, comprehending all the various soils and climates of the world, and abounding with all the necessaries and conveniences of life, are now, by the late satisfactory pacification, acknowledged to be possessed of absolute freedom and independency. They are, from this period, to be considered as the actors on a most conspicuous theatre, which seems to be peculiarly designated by Providence for the display of human greatness and felicity. Here they are not only surrounded with every thing, which can contribute to the completion of private and domestic enjoyment; but Heaven has crowned all its other blessings, by giving a fairer opportunity for political happiness, than any other nation has ever been favored with. Nothing can illustrate these observations more forcibly, than a recollection of the happy conjuncture of times and circumstances, under which our republic assumed its rank among the nations. The foundation of our empire was not laid in the gloomy age of ignorance and superstition; but at an epocha when the rights of mankind were better understood and more clearly defined, than at any former period. The researches of the human mind after social happiness have been carried to a great extent; the treasures of knowledge, acquired by the labors of philosophers, sages, and legislators, through a long succession of years, are laid open for our use, and their collected wisdom may be happily applied in the establishment of our forms of government. The free cultivation of letters, the unbounded extension of commerce, the progressive refinement of manners, the growing liberality of sentiment, and, above all, the pure and benign light of Revelation, have had a meliorating influence on mankind and increased the blessings of society. At this auspicious period, the United States came into existence as a nation; and, if their citizens should not be completely free and happy, the fault will be entirely their own.

Such is our situation, and such are our prospects; but notwithstanding the cup of blessing is thus reached out to us; notwithstanding happiness is ours, if we have a disposition to seize the occasion and make it our own; yet it appears to me there is an option still left to the United States of America, that it is in their choice, and depends upon their conduct, whether they will be respectable and prosperous, or contemptible and miserable, as a nation. This is the time of their political probation; this is the moment when the eyes of the whole world are turned upon them; this is the moment to establish or ruin their national character for ever; this is the favorable moment to give such a tone to our federal government, as will enable it to answer the ends of its institution, or this may be the ill-fated moment for relaxing the powers of the Union, annihilating the cement of the confederation, and exposing us to become the sport of European politics, which may play one State against another, to prevent their growing importance, and to serve their own interested purposes. For, according to the system of policy the States shall adopt at this moment, they will stand or fall; and by their confirmation or lapse it is yet to be decided, whether the revolution must ultimately be considered as a blessing or a curse; a blessing or a curse, not to the present age alone, for with our fate will the destiny of unborn millions be involved.

With this conviction of the importance of the present crisis, silence in me would be a crime. I will therefore speak to your Excellency the language of freedom and of sincerity without disguise. I am aware, however, that those who differ from me in political sentiment, may perhaps remark, I am stepping out of the proper line of my duty, and may possibly ascribe to arrogance or ostentation, what I know is alone the result of the purest intention. But the rectitude of my own heart, which disdains such unworthy motives; the part I have hitherto acted in life; the determination I have formed, of not taking any share in public business hereafter; the ardent desire I feel, and shall continue to manifest, of quietly enjoying, in private life, after all the toils of war, the benefits of a wise and liberal government, will, I flatter myself, sooner or latter convince my countrymen, that I could have no sinister views in delivering, with so little reserve, the opinions contained in this address.

There are four things, which, I humbly conceive, are essential to the well-being, I may even venture to say, to the existence of the United States, as an independent power.

First. An indissoluble union of the States under one federal head.

Secondly. A sacred regard to public justice.

Thirdly. The adoption of a proper peace establishment; and,

Fourthly. The prevalence of that pacific and friendly disposition among the people of the United States, which will induce them to forget their local prejudices and policies; to make those mutual concessions, which are requisite to the general prosperity; and, in some instances, to sacrifice their individual advantages to the interest of the community.

These are the pillars on which the glorious fabric of our independency and national character must be supported. Liberty is the basis; and whoever would dare to sap the foundation, or overturn the structure, under whatever specious pretext he may attempt it, will merit the bitterest execration, and the severest punishment, which can be inflicted by his injured country.

On the three first articles I will make a few observations, leaving the last to the good sense and serious consideration of those immediately concerned.

Under the first head, although it may not be necessary or proper for me, in this place, to enter into a particular disquisition on the principles of the Union, and to take up the great question which has been frequently agitated, whether it be expedient and requisite for the States to delegate a larger proportion of power to Congress, or not; yet it will be a part of my duty, and that of every true patriot, to assert without reserve, and to insist upon, the following positions. That, unless the States will suffer Congress to exercise those prerogatives they are undoubtedly invested with by the constitution, every thing must very rapidly tend to anarchy and confusion. That it is indispensable to the happiness of the individual States, that there should be lodged somewhere a supreme power to regulate and govern the general concerns of the confederated republic, without which the Union cannot be of long duration. That there must be a faithful and pointed compliance, on the part of every State, with the late proposals and demands of Congress, or the most fatal consequences will ensue. That whatever measures have a tendency to dissolve the Union, or contribute to violate or lessen the sovereign authority, ought to be considered as hostile to the liberty and independency of America, and the authors of them treated accordingly. And lastly, that unless we can be enabled, by the concurrence of the States, to participate of the fruits of the revolution, and enjoy the essential benefits of civil society, under a form of government so free and uncorrupted, so happily guarded against the danger of oppression, as has been devised and adopted by the articles of confederation, it will be a subject of regret, that so much blood and treasure have been lavished for no purpose, that so many sufferings have been encountered without a compensation, and that so many sacrifices have been made in vain.

Many other considerations might here be adduced to prove, that, without an entire conformity to the spirit of the Union, we cannot exist as an independent power. It will be sufficient for my purpose to mention but one or two, which seem to me of the greatest importance. It is only in our united character, as an empire, that our independence is acknowledged, that our power can be regarded, or our credit supported, among foreign nations. The treaties of the European powers with the United States of America will have no validity on a dissolution of the Union. We shall be left nearly in a state of nature; or we may find, by our own unhappy experience, that there is a natural and necessary progression from the extreme of anarchy to the extreme of tyranny, and that arbitrary power is most easily established on the ruins of liberty, abused to licentiousness.

As to the second article, which respects the performance of public justice, Congress have, in their late address to the United States, almost exhausted the subject; they have explained their ideas so fully, and have enforced the obligations the States are under, to render complete justice to all the public creditors, with so much dignity and energy, that, in my opinion, no real friend to the honor of independency of America can hesitate a single moment, respecting the propriety of complying with the just and honorable measures proposed. If their arguments do not produce conviction, I know of nothing that will have greater influence: especially when we recollect, that the system referred to, being the result of the collected wisdom of the continent, must be esteemed, if not perfect, certainly the least objectionable of any that could be devised; and that, if it shall not be carried into immediate execution, a national bankruptcy, with all its deplorable consequences, will take place, before any different plan can possibly be proposed and adopted. So pressing are the present circumstances, and such is the alternative now offered to the States.

The ability of the country to discharge the debts, which have been incurred in its defence, is not to be doubted; an inclination, I flatter myself, will not be wanting. The path of our duty is plain before us; honesty will be found, on every experiment, to be the best and only true policy. Let us then, as a nation, be just; let us fulfil the public contracts, which Congress had undoubtedly a right to make for the purpose of carrying on the war, with the same good faith we suppose ourselves bound to perform our private engagements. In the mean time, let an attention to the cheerful performance of their proper business, as individuals and as members of society, be earnestly inculcated on the citizens of America; then will they strengthen the hands of government, and be happy under its protection; every one will reap the fruit of his labors, every one will enjoy his own acquisitions, without molestation and without danger.

In this state of absolute freedom and perfect security, who will grudge to yield a very little of his property to support the common interest of society, and insure the protection of government? Who does not remember the frequent declarations, at the commencement of the war, that we should be completely satisfied, if, at the expense of one half, we could defend the remainder of our possessions? Where is the man to be found, who wishes to remain indebted for the defence of his own person and property to the exertions, the bravery, and the blood of others, without making one generous effort to repay the debt of honor and gratitude? In what part of the continent shall we find any man, or body of men, who would not blush to stand up and propose measures purposely calculated to rob the soldier of his stipend, and the public creditor of his due? And were it possible, that such a flagrant instance of injustice could ever happen, would it not excite the general indignation, and tend to bring down upon the authors of such measures the aggravated vengeance of Heaven? If, after all, a spirit of disunion, or a temper of obstinacy and perverseness should manifest itself in any of the States; if such an ungracious disposition should attempt to frustrate all the happy effects that might be expected to flow from the Union; if there should be a refusal to comply with the requisition for funds to discharge the annual interest of the public debts; and if that refusal should revive again all those jealousies, and produce all those evils, which are now happily removed, Congress, who have, in all their transactions, shown a great degree of magnanimity and justice, will stand justified in the sight of God and man; and the State alone, which puts itself in opposition to the aggregate wisdom of the continent, and follows such mistaken and pernicious counsels, will be responsible for all the consequences.

For my own part, conscious of having acted, while a servant of the public, in the manner I conceived best suited to promote the real interests of my country; having, in consequence of my fixed belief, in some measure pledged myself to the army, that their country would finally do them complete and ample justice; and not wishing to conceal any instance of my official conduct from the eyes of the world, I have thought proper to transmit to your Excellency the enclosed collection of papers, relative to the half-pay and commutation granted by Congress to the officers of the army. From these communications, my decided sentiments will be clearly comprehended, together with the conclusive reasons which induced me, at an early period, to recommend the adoption of this measure, in the most earnest and serious manner. As the proceedings of Congress, the army, and myself, are open to all, and contain, in my opinion, sufficient information to remove the prejudices and errors, which may have been entertained by any, I think it unnecessary to say any thing more than just to observe, that the resolutions of Congress, now alluded to, are undoubtedly as absolutely binding upon the United States, as the most solemn acts of confederation or legislation.

As to the idea, which, I am informed, has in some instances prevailed, that the half-pay and commutation are to be regarded merely in the odious light of a pension, it ought to be exploded for ever. That provision should be viewed, as it really was, a reasonable compensation offered by Congress, at a time when they had nothing else to give to the officers of the army for services then to be performed. It was the only means to prevent a total dereliction of the service. It was a part of their hire. I may be allowed to say, it was the price of their blood, and of your independency; it is therefore more than a common debt, it is a debt of honor; it can never be considered as a pension or gratuity, nor be cancelled until it is fairly discharged.

With regard to a distinction between officers and soldiers, it is sufficient that the uniform experience of every nation of the world, combined with our own, proves the utility and propriety of the discrimination. Rewards, in proportion to the aids the public derives from them, are unquestionably due to all its servants. In some lines, the soldiers have perhaps generally had as ample a compensation for their services, by the large bounties which have been paid to them, as their officers will receive in the proposed commutation; in others, if, besides the donation of lands, the payment of arrearages of clothing and wages (in which articles all the component parts of the army must be put upon the same footing), we take into the estimate the douceurs many of the soldiers have received, and the gratuity of one year's full pay, which is promised to all, possibly their situation (every circumstance being duly considered) will not be deemed less eligible than that of the officers. Should a further reward, however, be judged equitable, I will venture to assert, no one will enjoy greater satisfaction than myself, on seeing an exemption from taxes for a limited time, (which has been petitioned for in some instances,) or any other adequate immunity or compensation granted to the brave defenders of their country's cause; but neither the adoption or rejection of this proposition will in any manner affect, much less militate against, the act of Congress, by which they have offered five years' full pay, in lieu of the half-pay for life, which had been before promised to the officers of the army.

Before I conclude the subject of public justice, I cannot omit to mention the obligations this country is under to that meritorious class of veteran non-commissioned officers and privates, who have been discharged for inability, in consequence of the resolution of Congress of the 23d of April, 1782, on an annual pension for life. Their peculiar sufferings, their singular merits, and claims to that provision, need only be known, to interest all the feelings of humanity in their behalf. Nothing but a punctual payment of their annual allowance can rescue them from the most complicated misery; and nothing could be a more melancholy and distressing sight, than to behold those, who have shed their blood or lost their limbs in the service of their country, without a shelter, without a friend, and without the means of obtaining any of the necessaries or comforts of life, compelled to beg their daily bread from door to door. Suffer me to recommend those of this description, belonging to your State, to the warmest patronage of your Excellency and your legislature.

It is necessary to say but a few words on the third topic which was proposed, and which regards particularly the defence of the republic; as there can be little doubt but Congress will recommend a proper peace establishment for the United States, in which a due attention will be paid to the importance of placing the militia of the Union upon a regular and respectable footing. If this should be the case, I would beg leave to urge the great advantage of it in the strongest terms. The militia of this country must be considered as the palladium of our security, and the first effectual resort in case of hostility. It is essential, therefore, that the same system should pervade the whole; that the formation and discipline of the militia of the continent should be absolutely uniform, and that the same species of arms, accoutrements, and military apparatus, should be introduced in every part of the United States. No one, who has not learned it from experience, can conceive the difficulty, expense, and confusion, which result from a contrary system, or the vague arrangements which have hitherto prevailed.

If, in treating of political points, a greater latitude than usual has been taken in the course of this address, the importance of the crisis, and the magnitude of the objects in discussion, must be my apology. It is, however, neither my wish or expectation, that the preceding observations should claim any regard, except so far as they shall appear to be dictated by a good intention, consonant to the immutable rules of justice, calculated to produce a liberal system of policy, and founded on whatever experience may have been acquired by a long and close attention to public business. Here I might speak with the more confidence, from my actual observations; and, if it would not swell this letter (already too prolix) beyond the bounds I had prescribed to myself, I could demonstrate to every mind open to conviction, that in less time, and with much less expense, than has been incurred, the war might have been brought to the same happy conclusion, if the resources of the continent could have been properly drawn forth; that the distresses and disappointments, which have very often occurred, have, in too many instances, resulted more from a want of energy in the Continental government, than a deficiency of means in the particular States; that the inefficacy of measures arising from the want of an adequate authority in the supreme power, from a partial compliance with the requisitions of Congress in some of the States, and from a failure of punctuality in others, while it tended to damp the zeal of those, which were more willing to exert themselves, served also to accumulate the expenses of the war, and to frustrate the best concerted plans; and that the discouragement occasioned by the complicated difficulties and embarrassments, in which our affairs were by this means involved, would have long ago produced the dissolution of any army, less patient, less virtuous, and less persevering, than that which I have had the honor to command. But, while I mention these things, which are notorious facts, as the defects of our federal constitution, particularly in the prosecution of a war, I beg it may be understood, that, as I have ever taken a pleasure in gratefully acknowledging the assistance and support I have derived from every class of citizens, so shall I always be happy to do justice to the unparalleled exertions of the individual States on many interesting occasions.

I have thus freely disclosed what I wished to make known, before I surrendered up my public trust to those who committed it to me. The task is now accomplished. I now bid adieu to your Excellency as the chief magistrate of your State, at the same time I bid a last farewell to the cares of office, and all the employments of public life.

It remains, then, to be my final and only request, that your Excellency will communicate these sentiments to your legislature at their next meeting, and that they may be considered as the legacy of one, who has ardently wished, on all occasions, to be useful to his country, and who, even in the shade of retirement, will not fail to implore the Divine benediction upon it.

I now make it my earnest prayer, that God would have you, and the State over which you preside, in his holy protection; that he would incline the hearts of the citizens to cultivate a spirit of subordination and obedience to government; to entertain a brotherly affection and love for one another, for their fellow citizens of the United States at large, and particularly for their brethren who have served in the field; and finally, that he would most graciously be pleased to dispose us all to do justice, to love mercy, and to demean ourselves with that charity, humility, and pacific temper of mind, which were the characteristics of the Divine Author of our blessed religion, and without an humble imitation of whose example in these things, we can never hope to be a happy nation.

I have the honor to be, with much esteem and respect, Sir, your Excellency's most obedient and most humble servant.

SECTION TWO:
THE PRESIDENTIAL YEARS

WASHINGTON'S FIRST INAUGURAL ADDRESS, APRIL 30, 1789

George Washington's First Inaugural Address
Given in New York, on Thursday, April 30, 1789

Fellow-Citizens of the Senate and of the House of Representatives:

Among the vicissitudes incident to life no event could have filled me with greater anxieties than that of which the notification was transmitted by your order, and received on the 14th day of the present month.

On the one hand, I was summoned by my country, whose voice I can never hear but with veneration and love, from a retreat which I had chosen with the fondest predilection, and, in my flattering hopes, with an immutable decision, as the asylum of my declining years—a retreat which was rendered every day more necessary as well as more dear to me by the addition of habit to inclination, and of frequent interruptions in my health to the gradual waste committed on it by time.

On the other hand, the magnitude and difficulty of the trust to which the voice of my country called me, being sufficient to awaken in the wisest and most experienced of her citizens a distrustful scrutiny into his qualifications, could not but overwhelm with despondence one who (inheriting inferior endowments from nature and unpracticed in the duties of civil administration) ought to be peculiarly conscious of his own deficiencies. In this conflict of emotions all I dare aver is that it has been my faithful study to collect my duty from a just appreciation of every circumstance by which it might be affected. All I dare hope is that if, in executing this task, I have been too much swayed by a grateful remembrance of former instances, or by an affectionate sensibility to this transcendent proof of the confidence of my fellow-citizens, and have thence too little consulted my incapacity as well as disinclination for the weighty and untried cares before me, my error will be palliated by the motives which mislead me, and its consequences be judged by my country with some share of the partiality in which they originated.

Such being the impressions under which I have, in obedience to the public summons, repaired to the present station, it would be peculiarly improper to omit in this first official act my fervent supplications to that Almighty Being who rules over the universe, who presides in the councils of nations, and whose providential aids can supply every human defect, that His benediction may consecrate to the liberties and happiness of the people of the United States a Government instituted by themselves for these essential purposes, and may enable every instrument employed in its administration to execute with success the functions allotted to his charge. In tendering this homage to the Great Author of every public and private good, I assure myself that it expresses your sentiments not less than my own, nor those of my fellow-citizens at large less than either. No people can be bound to acknowledge and adore the Invisible Hand which conducts the affairs of men more than those of the United States. Every step by which they have advanced to the character of an independent nation seems to have been distinguished by some token of providential agency; and in the important revolution just accomplished in the system of their united government the tranquil deliberations and voluntary consent of so many distinct communities from which the event has resulted can not be compared with the means by which most governments have been established without some return of pious gratitude, along with an humble anticipation of the future blessings which the past seem to presage. These reflections, arising out of the present crisis, have forced themselves too strongly on my mind to be suppressed. You will join with me, I trust, in thinking that there are none under the influence of which the proceedings of a new and free government can more auspiciously commence.

By the article establishing the executive department it is made the duty of the President "to recommend to your consideration such measures as he shall judge necessary and expedient." The circumstances under which I now meet you will acquit me from entering into that subject further than to refer to the great constitutional charter under which you are assembled, and which, in defining your powers, designates the objects to which your attention is to be given. It will be more consistent with those circumstances, and far more congenial with the feelings which actuate me, to substitute, in place of a recommendation of particular measures, the tribute that is due to the talents, the rectitude, and the patriotism which adorn the characters selected to devise and adopt them. In these honorable qualifications I behold the surest pledges that as on one side no local prejudices or attachments, no separate views nor party animosities, will misdirect the comprehensive and equal eye which ought to watch over this great assemblage of communities and interests, so, on another, that the foundation of our national policy will be laid in the pure and immutable principles of private morality, and the preeminence of free government be exemplified by all the attributes which can win the affections of its citizens and command the respect of the world. I dwell on this prospect with every satisfaction which an ardent love for my country can inspire, since there is no truth more thoroughly established than that there exists in the economy and course of nature an indissoluble union between virtue and happiness; between duty and advantage; between the genuine maxims of an honest and magnanimous policy and the solid rewards of public prosperity and felicity; since we ought to be no less persuaded that the propitious smiles of Heaven can never be expected on a nation that disregards the eternal rules of order and right which Heaven itself has ordained; and since the preservation of the sacred fire of liberty and the destiny of the republican model of government are justly considered, perhaps, as 'deeply', as 'finally', staked on the experiment entrusted to the hands of the American people.

Besides the ordinary objects submitted to your care, it will remain with your judgment to decide how far an exercise of the occasional power delegated by the fifth article of the Constitution is rendered expedient at the present juncture by the nature of objections which have been urged against the system, or by the degree of inquietude which has given birth to them. Instead of undertaking particular recommendations on this subject, in which I could be guided by no lights derived from official opportunities, I shall again give way to my entire confidence in your discernment and pursuit of the public good; for I assure myself that whilst you carefully avoid every alteration which might endanger the benefits of an united and effective government, or which ought to await the future lessons of experience, a reverence for the characteristic rights of freemen and a regard for the public harmony will sufficiently influence your deliberations on the question how far the former can be impregnably fortified or the latter be safely and advantageously promoted.

To the foregoing observations I have one to add, which will be most properly addressed to the House of Representatives. It concerns myself, and will therefore be as brief as possible. When

I was first honored with a call into the service of my country, then on the eve of an arduous struggle for its liberties, the light in which I contemplated my duty required that I should renounce every pecuniary compensation. From this resolution I have in no instance departed; and being still under the impressions which produced it, I must decline as inapplicable to myself any share in the personal emoluments which may be indispensably included in a permanent provision for the executive department, and must accordingly pray that the pecuniary estimates for the station in which I am placed may during my continuance in it be limited to such actual expenditures as the public good may be thought to require.

Having thus imparted to you my sentiments as they have been awakened by the occasion which brings us together, I shall take my present leave; but not without resorting once more to the benign Parent of the Human Race in humble supplication that, since He has been pleased to favor the American people with opportunities for deliberating in perfect tranquillity, and dispositions for deciding with unparalleled unanimity on a form of government for the security of their union and the advancement of their happiness, so His divine blessing may be equally 'conspicuous' in the enlarged views, the temperate consultations, and the wise measures on which the success of this Government must depend.

TO THE BISHOPS, CLERGY, AND LAITY OF THE PROTESTANT EPISCOPAL CHURCH, AUGUST 19, 1789

To the Bishops, Clergy, and Laity of the Protestant Episcopal Church in the States of New York, New Jersey, Pennsylvania, Delaware, Maryland, Virginia, and North Carolina, in General Convention Assembled.

19 August, 1789

I sincerely thank you for your affectionate congratulations on my election to the chief magistracy of the United States. After having received from my fellow-citizens in general the most liberal treatment, after having found them disposed to contemplate, in the most flattering point of view, the performance of my military services, and the manner of my retirement at the close of the war, I feel that I have a right to console myself in my present arduous undertakings with a hope that they will still be inclined to put the most favorable construction on the motives, which may influence me in my future public transactions.

The satisfaction arising from the indulgent opinion entertained by the American people of my conduct will, I trust, be some security for preventing me from doing anything, which might justly incur the forfeiture of that opinion. And the consideration, that human happiness and moral duty are inseparably connected, will always continue to prompt me to promote the progress of the former by inculcating the practice of the latter.

On this occasion, it would ill become me to conceal the joy I have felt in perceiving the fraternal affection, which appears to increase every day among the friends of genuine religion. It affords edifying prospects, indeed, to see Christians of different denominations dwell together in more charity, and conduct themselves in respect to each other with a more Christian-like spirit, than ever they have done in any former age, or in any other nation.

I receive with the greater satisfaction your congratulations on the establishment of the new constitution of government, because I believe its mild yet efficient operations will tend to remove every remaining apprehension of those, with whose opinions it may not entirely coincide, as well as to confirm the hopes of its numerous friends; and because the moderation, patriotism, and wisdom of the present federal legislature seem to promise the restoration of order and our ancient virtues, the extension of genuine religion, and the consequent advancement of our respectability abroad, and of our substantial happiness at home.

I request, most reverend and respected gentlemen, that you will accept my cordial thanks for your devout supplications to the

Supreme Ruler of the Universe in behalf of me.
May you, and the people whom you represent,
be the happy subjects of the divine benedictions
both here and hereafter.

LETTER TO CATHARINE MACAULAY GRAHAM, JANUARY 9, 1790

To Catharine Macaulay Graham.
New York,
9 January, 1790.

Madam,

Your obliging letter dated in October last has been received, and, as I do not know when I shall have more leisure than at present to throw together a few observations in return for yours, I take up my pen to do it by this early occasion.

In the first place I thank you for your congratulatory sentiments on the event, which has placed me at the head of the American government, as well as for the indulgent partiality, which it is to be feared, however, may have warped your judgment too much in my favor. But you do me no more than justice in supposing, that, if I had been permitted to indulge my first and fondest wish, I should have remained in a private station.

Although neither the present age nor posterity may possibly give me full credit for the feelings, which I have experienced on this subject, yet I have a consciousness that nothing short of an absolute conviction of duty could ever have brought me upon the scenes of public life again. The establishment of our new government seemed to be the last great experiment for promoting human happiness by a reasonable compact in civil society. It was to be in the first instance, in a considerable degree, a government of accommodation as well as a government of laws. Much was to be done by prudence, much by conciliation, much by firmness. Few, who are not philosophical spectators, can realize the difficult and delicate part, which a man in my situation had to act. All see, and most admire, the glare which hovers round the external happiness of elevated office. To me there is nothing in it beyond the lustre, which may be reflected from its connexion with a power of promoting human felicity.

In our progress towards political happiness my station is new, and, if I may use the expression, I walk on untrodden ground. There is scarcely an action, the motive to which may not be subject to a double interpretation. There is scarcely any part of my conduct, which may not hereafter be drawn into precedent. Under such a view of the duties inherent to my arduous office, I could not but feel a diffidence in myself on the one hand, and an anxiety for the community, that every new arrangement should be made in the best possible manner, on the other. If, after all my humble but faithful endeavors to advance the felicity of my country and mankind, I may indulge a hope that my labors have not been altogether without success, it will be the only real compensation I can receive in the closing scenes of life.

On the actual situation of this country under its new government, I will, in the next place, make a few remarks. That the government, though not actually perfect, is one of the best in the world, I have little doubt. I always believed, that an unequivocally free and equal representation of the people in the legislature, together with an efficient and responsible executive, were the great pillars on which the preservation of American freedom must depend. It was indeed next to a miracle, that there should have been so much unanimity in points of such importance among such a number of citizens, so widely scattered, and so different in their habits in many respects, as the Americans were. Nor are the growing unanimity and increasing good will of the citizens to the government less remarkable, than favorable circumstances. So far as we have gone with the new government, (and it is completely organized and in operation,) we have had greater reason, than the most sanguine could expect, to be satisfied with its success. Perhaps a number of accidental circumstances have concurred with the real effects of the government to make the people uncommonly well pleased with their situation and prospects. The harvests of wheat have been remarkably good, the demand for that article from abroad is great, the increase of commerce is visible in every port, and the number of new manufactures introduced in one year is astonishing. I have lately made a tour through the eastern States. I found the country in a great degree recovered from the ravages of war; the Towns flourishing, and the people delighted with a government instituted by themselves, and for their own good. The same facts I have also reason to believe, from good authority, exist in the southern States.

By what I have just observed, I think you will be persuaded, that the ill-boding politicians, who prognosticated that America never would enjoy any fruits from her independence, and that she would be obliged to have recourse to a foreign power for protection, have at least been mistaken. I shall sincerely rejoice to see, that the American revolution has been productive of happy consequences on both sides of the Atlantic. The renovation of the French constitution is indeed one of the most wonderful events in the history of mankind, and the agency of the Marquis de Lafayette in a high degree honorable to his character. My greatest fear has been, that the nation would not be sufficiently cool and moderate in making arrangements for the security of that liberty, of which it seems to be fully possessed.

Mr. Warville, the French gentleman you mention, has been in America and at Mount Vernon, but has returned some time since to France. Mrs. Washington is well, and desires her compliments may be presented to you. We wish the happiness of your fireside, as we also long to enjoy that of our own at Mount Vernon. Our wishes, you know were limited, and I think that our plans of living will now be deemed reasonable by the considerate part of our species. Her wishes coincide with my own, as to simplicity of dress, and every thing which can tend to support propriety of character, without partaking of the follies of luxury and ostentation. I am with great regard, &c.

WASHINGTON'S SECOND INAUGURAL ADDRESS, MARCH 4, 1793

Fellow-Citizens:

I am again called upon by the voice of my Country to execute the functions of its Chief Magistrate. When the occasion proper for it shall arrive, I shall endeavour to express the high sense I entertain of this distinguished honor, and of the confidence which has been reposed in me by the people of United America.

Previous to the execution of any official act of the President, the Constitution requires an Oath of Office. This Oath I am now about to take, and in your presence, that if it shall be found during my administration of the Government I have in any instance violated willingly, or knowingly, the injunction thereof, I may (besides incurring

Constitutional punishment) be subject to the upbraidings of all who are now witnesses of the present solemn Ceremony.

George Washington

PROCLAMATION OF NEUTRALITY, APRIL 22, 1793

Whereas it appears that a state of war exists between Austria, Prussia, Sardinia, Great Britain, and the United Netherlands, on the one part, and France on the other; and the duty and interest of the United States require, that they should with sincerity and good faith adopt and pursue a conduct friendly and impartial towards the belligerent powers:

I have therefore thought fit by these presents, to declare the disposition of the United States to observe the conduct aforesaid towards those powers respectively; and to exhort and warn the citizens of the United States carefully to avoid all acts and proceedings whatsoever, which may in any manner tend to contravene such disposition.

And I do hereby also make known, that whosoever of the citizens of the United States shall render himself liable to punishment or forfeiture under the law of nations, by committing, aiding or abetting hostilities against any of the said powers, or by carrying to any of them, those articles which are deemed contraband by the modern usage of nations, will not receive the protection of the United States against such punishment or forfeiture; and further that I have given instructions to those officers to whom it belongs, to cause prosecutions to be instituted against all persons, who shall, within the cognizance of the Courts of the United States, violate the law of nations, with respect to the powers at war, or any of them.

LETTER TO JOHN H. STONE, GOVERNOR OF MARYLAND, DECEMBER 6, 1795

To John H. Stone, Governor of Maryland.
Philadelphia,
6 December, 1795

Dear Sir:
By Thursday's post I was favored with your letter of the 27th ultimo, enclosing a Declaration of the General Assembly of Maryland. At any time the expression of such a sentiment would have been considered as highly honorable and flattering. At the present, when the voice of malignancy is so high-toned, and no attempts are left unessayed to destroy all confidence in the constituted authorities of this country, it is peculiarly grateful

to my sensibility; and, coming spontaneously, and with the unanimity it has done from so respectable a representation of the people, it adds weight as well as pleasure to the act.

I have long since resolved, for the present time at least, to let my calumniators proceed without any notice being taken of their invectives by myself, or by any others with my participation or knowledge. Their views, I dare say, are readily perceived by all the enlightened and well-disposed part of the community; and by the records of my administration, and not by the voice of faction, I expect to be acquitted or condemned hereafter.

For your politeness in making the unofficial and friendly communication of this act, I pray you to receive my thanks, and assurances at the same time of my being, with very great esteem and regard,

dear Sir,
&c.

LETTER TO GOUVERNEUR MORRIS, SENATOR OF PENNSYLVANIA, DECEMBER 22, 1795

To Gouverneur Morris.
Philadelphia,
22 December, 1795

My dear Sir,

I am become so unprofitable a correspondent, and so remiss in my correspondencies, that nothing but the kindness of my friends, in overlooking these deficiencies, could induce them to favor me with a continuance of their letters; which to me are at once pleasing, interesting, and useful. To a man immersed in debt, and seeing no prospect of extrication but by an act of insolvency (perhaps absolvency would be a better word), I compare myself; and like him, too, afraid to examine the items of the account, I will at once make a lumping acknowledgment of the receipt of many interesting private letters from you, previous to your last arrival in England, and will begin with those subsequent thereto of the 3d of July and 22d of August.

As the British government has repealed the order for seizing our provision vessels, little more need be said on that head, than that it was the *principle,* which constituted the most obnoxious and exceptionable part thereof, and the predicament in which this country was thereby placed in her relations with France. Admitting, therefore, that the compensation to *some* individuals was adequate to what it might have been in another quarter, yet the exceptions to it on these grounds remained the same.

I do not think Colonel Innes's report to the governor of Kentucky was entirely free from exceptions. But let the report be accompanied with the following remarks. 1, that the one, which Lord Grenville might have seen published, was disclaimed by Colonel Innes, as soon as it appeared in the public gazettes, on account of its incorrectness. 2, an irritable spirit at that time pervaded all our people at the westward, arising from a combination of causes (but from none more powerful, than the analogous proceedings of Great Britain in the north, with those of Spain in the south, towards the United States and their Indian borderers), which spirit required some management and soothing. But, 3d and principally, Lord Grenville if he had adverted to the many remonstrances, which have gone from this country against the conduct of his own, which I will take the liberty to say has been as impolitic for their nation, (if peace and a good understanding with this was its object,) as it has been irritating to us. And, that it may not be conceived I am speaking at random, let his Lordship be asked, if we have not complained,—That some of their naval officers have insulted and menaced us in *our own ports?* That they have violated our national rights, by searching vessels and impressing seamen within our acknowledged jurisdiction, and in an outrageous manner have seized the latter by *entire crews* in the West Indies, and done the like, but not so extensively, in all parts of the world? That the Bermudian privateers, or to speak more correctly, pirates, and the admiralty court of that island, have committed the most atrocious depredations and violences on our commerce, in capturing, and in their adjudications afterwards, as were never tolerated in any well-organized or efficient government? That their governor of Upper Canada has ordered in an official and formal manner settlers within our own territory, (and far removed from the posts they have withheld from us,) to withdraw, and forbid others to settle on the same? That the persons, to whom their Indian affairs are intrusted, have taken unwearied pains and practised every deception to keep those people in a state of irritation and disquietude with us; and, to the *latest* moment, exerted every nerve to prevent the treaty, which has lately been concluded between the United States and them from taking effect?

These complaints were not founded in vague and idle reports, but on indubitable facts; facts, not only known to the government, but so notorious as to be known to the people also, who charge to the last item of the above enumeration the expenditure of a million or more of dollars annually for the purpose of self-defence against Indian tribes thus stimulated, and for chastising them for the ravages and cruel murders, which they had committed on our frontier inhabitants. Our minister at the court of London has been directed to remonstrate against these things with force and energy. The answer, it is true, has been (particularly with respect to the interferences with the Indians) a disavowal. Why then are not the agents of such unauthorized, offensive, and injurious measures made examples of? For wherein, let me ask, consists the difference *to us* between their being the acts of government, or the acts of unauthorized officers or agents of the government, if we are to sustain all the evils, which flow from such measures?

To this catalogue may be added the indifference, nay, more than indifference, with which the government of Great Britain received the advances of this country towards a friendly intercourse with it, even after the adoption of the present constitution, and since the operation of the government; and, also, the ungracious and obnoxious characters, (rancorous refugees, as if done with design to insult the country,) which they have sent among us as their agents, who, retaining all their former enmity, could see nothing through a proper medium, and becoming the earwigs of their minister (who, by the by, does not possess a mind capacious enough, or a temper sufficiently conciliatory, to view things and act upon a great and liberal scale), were always laboring under some unfavorable information and impression, and probably not communicating them in a less exceptionable manner than they received or conceived them themselves.

I give you these details (and, if you should again converse with Lord Grenville on the subject you are at liberty, unofficially to mention them, or any of them, according to circumstances), as evidences of the impolitic conduct (for so it strikes me) of the British government towards these United States; that it may be seen how difficult it has been for the executive, under such an accumulation of irritating circumstances, to maintain the ground of neutrality, which had been taken; at a time when the remembrance of the aid we had received from France in the revolution was fresh in every mind, and when the partisans of that country were continually contrasting the affections of *that* people with the unfriendly disposition of the *British government*. And that, too, as I have observed before, while the recollection of *their own* sufferings during the war with the latter had not been forgotten.

It is well known, that peace (to borrow a modern phrase) has been the order of the day with me since the disturbances in Europe first commenced, My policy has been, and will continue to be, while I have the honor to remain in the administration of the government, to be upon friendly terms with, but independent of, all the nations of the earth; to share in the broils of none; to fulfil our own engagements; to supply the wants and be carrier for them all; being thoroughly convinced, that it is our policy and interest to do so. Nothing short of self-respect, and that justice which is essential to a national character, ought to involve us in war; for sure I am, if this country is preserved in tranquillity twenty years longer, it may bid defiance in a just cause to any power whatever; such in that time will be its population, wealth, and resources.

If Lord Grenville conceives, that the United States are not well disposed towards Great Britain, his candor, I am persuaded, will seek for the causes, and his researches will fix them, as I have done. If this should be the case, his policy will I am persuaded be opposed to the continuance or renewal of the irritating measures, which I have enumerated; for he may be assured, (though the assurance will not, it is probable, carry conviction with it from me to a member of the British administration,) that a liberal policy will be one of the most effectual means of deriving advantages to their trade and manufactures from the people of the United States, and will contribute, more than any thing else, to obliterate the impressions, which have been made by their late conduct towards us.

In a government as free as ours, where the people are at liberty, and will express their sentiments oftentimes imprudently, and, for want of information, sometimes unjustly, allowances must be made for occasional effervescences; but, after the declaration which I have here made of my political creed, you can run no hazard in asserting, that the executive branch of this government never has, or will suffer, while I preside, any improper conduct of its officers to escape with impunity, or will give its sanctions to any disorderly proceedings of its citizens.

By a firm adherence to these principles, and to the neutral policy which has been adopted, I have brought on myself a torrent of abuse in the factious papers in this country, and from the enmity of the discontented of all descriptions therein. But, having no sinister objects in view, I shall not be diverted from my course by these, nor any attempts which are, or shall be made to withdraw the confidence of my constituents from me. I have nothing to ask; and, discharging my duty, I have nothing to fear from invective. The acts of my administration will appear when

I am no more, and the intelligent and candid part of mankind will not condemn my conduct without recurring to them.

The treaty entered into with Great Britain has, as you have been informed, undergone much and severe animadversion; and, though a more favorable one were to have been wished, which the policy perhaps of Great Britain might have granted, yet the demerits thereof are not to be estimated by the opposition it has received; nor is the opposition sanctioned by the great body of the yeomanry in these States. For they, whatever their opinions of it may be, are disposed to leave the decision where the constitution has placed it. But an occasion was wanting, and the instrument, by those who required it, was deemed well calculated, for the purpose of working upon the affections of the people of this country towards those of France, whose interests and rights under our treaty with them they represented as being violated; and, with the aid of the provision order, and other irritating conduct of the British ships of war and agents, as mentioned before, the means were furnished, and more pains taken, than upon any former occasion, to raise a general ferment with a view to defeat the treaty.

But knowing that you have other correspondents, who have more leisure, and equally capable of detailing these matters, I will leave you to them and the gazettes for fuller information there and a more minute account of the prevailing politics. And thanking you for the interesting intelligence and opinions contained in your letter of the 22d of August, I shall only add, that, with sincere esteem and regard, I am, dear Sir, your affectionate friend.

P. S. We have not heard through any other channel than your Letter, of the intended resignation of Mr. Skipwith and of the proposed recommendation of Mr. Montflorence.

WASHINGTON'S FAREWELL ADDRESS, SEPTEMBER 19, 1796

The period for a new election of a citizen to administer the Executive Government of the United States being not far distant, and the time actually arrived when your thoughts must be employed in designating the person who is to be clothed with that important trust, it appears to me proper, especially as it may conduce to a more distinct expression of the public voice, that I should now apprise you of the resolution I have formed to decline being considered among the number of those out of whom a choice is to be made.

I beg you at the same time to do me the justice to be assured that this resolution has not been taken without a strict regard to all the considerations appertaining to the relation which binds a dutiful citizen to his country; and that in withdrawing the tender of service, which silence in my Situation might imply, I am influenced by no diminution of zeal for your future interest, no deficiency of grateful respect for your past kindness, but am supported by a full conviction that the step is compatible with both.

The acceptance of and continuance hitherto in the office to which your suffrages have twice called me have been a uniform sacrifice of inclination to the opinion of duty and to a deference for what appeared to be your desire. I constantly hoped that it would have been much earlier in my power, consistently with motives which I was not at liberty to disregard, to return to that retirement from which I had been reluctantly drawn. The strength of my inclination to do this previous to the last election had even led to the preparation of an address to declare it to you; but mature reflection on the then perplexed and critical posture of our affairs with foreign nations and the unanimous advice of persons entitled to my confidence impelled me to abandon the idea. I rejoice that the state of your concerns, external as well as internal, no longer renders the pursuit of inclination incompatible with the sentiment of duty or propriety, and am persuaded, whatever partiality may be retained for my services, that in the present circumstances of our country you will not disapprove my determination to retire.

The impressions with which I first undertook the arduous trust were explained on the proper occasion. In the discharge of this trust I will only say that I have, with good intentions, contributed toward the organization and administration of the Government the best exertions of which a very fallible judgment was capable, Not unconscious in the outset of the inferiority of my qualifications, experience in my own eyes, perhaps still more in the eyes of others, has strengthened the motives to diffidence of myself; and every day the increasing weight of years admonishes me more and more that the shade of retirement is as necessary to me as it will be welcome. Satisfied that if any circumstances have given peculiar value to my services they were temporary, I have the consolation to believe that, while choice and prudence invite me to quit the political scene, patriotism does not forbid it.

In looking forward to the moment which is intended to terminate the career of my political life my feelings do not permit me to suspend the deep acknowledgment of that debt of gratitude which I owe to my beloved country for the many honors it has conferred upon me; still more for the steadfast confidence with which it has supported me, and for the opportunities I have thence enjoyed of manifesting my inviolable attachment by services faithful and persevering, though in usefulness unequal to my zeal. If benefits have resulted to our country from these services, let it always be remembered to your praise and as an instructive example in our annals that under circumstances in which the passions, agitated in every direction, were liable to mislead; amidst appearances sometimes dubious; vicissitudes of fortune often discouraging; in situations in which not unfrequently want of success has countenanced the spirit of criticism, the constancy of your support was the essential prop of the efforts and a guaranty of the plans by which they were effected. Profoundly penetrated with this idea, I shall carry it with me to my grave as a strong incitement to unceasing vows that Heaven may continue to you the choicest tokens of its beneficence; that your union and brotherly affection may be perpetual; that the free Constitution which is the work of your hands may be sacredly maintained; that its administration in every department may be stamped with wisdom and virtue; that, in fine, the happiness of the people of these States, under the auspices of liberty, may be made complete by so careful a preservation and so prudent a use of this blessing as will acquire to them the glory of recommending it to the applause, the affection, and adoption of every nation which is yet a stranger to it.

Here, perhaps, I ought to stop. But a solicitude for your welfare which can not end but with my life, and the apprehension of danger natural to that solicitude, urge me on an occasion like the present to offer to your solemn contemplation and to recommend to your frequent review some sentiments which are the result of much reflection, of no inconsiderable observation, and which appear to me all important to the permanency of your felicity as a people. These will be offered to you with the more freedom as you can only see in them the disinterested warnings of a parting friend, who can possibly have no personal motive to bias his counsel. Nor can I forget as an encouragement to it your indulgent reception of my sentiments on a former and not dissimilar occasion.

Interwoven as is the love of liberty with every ligament of your hearts, no recommendation of mine is necessary to fortify or confirm the attachment.

The unity of government which constitutes you one people is also now dear to you. It is justly so, for it is a main pillar in the edifice of your real independence, the support of your tranquillity at home, your peace abroad, of your safety, of your prosperity, of that very liberty which you so highly prize. But as it is easy to foresee that from different causes and from different quarters much pains will be taken, many artifices employed, to weaken in your minds the conviction of this truth, as this is the point in your political fortress against which the batteries of internal and external enemies will be most constantly and actively (though often covertly and insidiously) directed, it is of infinite moment that you should properly estimate the immense value of your national union to your collective and individual happiness; that you should cherish a cordial, habitual, and immovable attachment to it; accustoming yourselves to think and speak of it as of the palladium of your political safety and prosperity; watching for its preservation with jealous anxiety; discountenancing whatever may suggest even a suspicion that it can in any event be abandoned, and indignantly frowning upon the first dawning of every attempt to alienate any portion of our country from the rest or to enfeeble the sacred ties which now link together the various parts.

For this you have every inducement of sympathy and interest. Citizens by birth or choice of a common country, that country has a right to concentrate your affections. The name of American, which belongs to you in your national capacity, must always exalt the just pride of patriotism more than any appellation derived from local discriminations. With slight shades of difference, you have the same religion, manners, habits, and political principles. You have in a common cause fought and triumphed together. The independence and liberty you possess are the work of joint councils and joint efforts, of common dangers, sufferings, and successes.

But these considerations, however powerfully they address themselves to your sensibility, are greatly outweighed by those which apply more immediately to your interest. Here every portion of our country finds the most commanding motives for carefully guarding and preserving the union of the whole.

The North, in an unrestrained intercourse with the South, protected by the equal laws of a common government, finds in the productions of the latter great additional resources of maritime and commercial enterprise and precious materials of manufacturing industry. The South, in the same intercourse, benefiting by the same agency of the North, sees its agriculture grow and its commerce expand. Turning partly into its own channels the seamen of the North, it finds its particular navigation invigorated; and while it contributes in different ways to nourish and increase the general mass of the national navigation, it looks forward to the protection of a maritime strength to which itself is unequally adapted. The East, in a like intercourse with the West, already finds, and in the progressive improvement of interior communications by land and water will more and more find, a valuable vent for the commodities which it brings from abroad or manufactures at home. The West derives from the East supplies requisite to its growth and comfort, and what is perhaps of still greater consequence, it must of necessity owe the secure enjoyment of indispensable outlets for its own productions to the weight, influence, and the future maritime strength of the Atlantic side of the Union, directed by an indissoluble community of interest as one nation. Any other tenure by which the West can hold this essential advantage, whether derived from its own separate strength or from an apostate and unnatural connection with any foreign power, must be intrinsically precarious.

While, then, every part of our country thus feels an immediate and particular interest in union, all the parts combined can not fail to find in the united mass of means and efforts greater strength, greater resource, proportionably greater security from external danger, a less frequent interruption of their peace by foreign nations, and what is of inestimable value, they must derive from union an exemption from those broils and wars between themselves which so frequently afflict neighboring countries not tied together by the same governments, which their own rivalships alone would be sufficient to produce, but which opposite foreign alliances, attachments, and intrigues would stimulate and imbitter. Hence, likewise, they will avoid the necessity of those overgrown military establishments which, under any form of government, are inauspicious to liberty, and which are to be regarded as particularly hostile to republican liberty. In this sense it is that your union ought to be considered as a main prop of your liberty, and that the love of the one ought to endear to you the preservation of the other.

These considerations speak a persuasive language to every reflecting and virtuous mind, and exhibit the continuance of the union as a primary object of patriotic desire. Is there a doubt whether a common government can embrace so large a sphere? Let experience solve it. To listen to mere speculation in such a case were criminal. We are authorized to hope that a proper organization of the whole, with the auxiliary agency of governments for the respective subdivisions, will afford a happy issue to the experiment. It is well worth a fair and full experiment. With such powerful and obvious motives to union affecting all parts of our country, while experience shall not have demonstrated its impracticability, there will always be reason to distrust the patriotism of those who in any quarter may endeavor to weaken its bands.

In contemplating the causes which may disturb our union it occurs as matter of serious concern that any ground should have been furnished for characterizing parties by geographical discriminations—Northern and Southern, Atlantic and Western— whence designing men may endeavor to excite a belief that there is a real difference of local interests and views. One of the expedients of party to acquire influence within particular districts is to misrepresent the opinions and aims of other districts. You can not shield yourselves too much against the jealousies and heartburnings which spring from these misrepresentations; they tend to render alien to each other those who ought to be bound together by fraternal affection. The inhabitants of our Western country have lately had a useful lesson on this head. They have seen in the negotiation by the Executive and in the unanimous ratification by the Senate of the treaty with Spain, and in the universal satisfaction at that event throughout the United States, a decisive proof how unfounded were the suspicions propagated among them of a policy in the General Government and in the Atlantic States unfriendly to their interests in regard to the Mississippi. They have been witnesses to the formation of two treaties that with Great

Britain and that with Spain—which secure to them everything they could desire in respect to our foreign relations toward confirming their prosperity. Will it not be their wisdom to rely for the preservation of these advantages on the union by which they were procured? Will they not henceforth be deaf to those advisers, if such there are, who would sever them from their brethren and connect them with aliens?

To the efficacy and permanency of your union a government for the whole is indispensable. No alliances, however strict, between the parts can be an adequate substitute. They must inevitably experience the infractions and interruptions which all alliances in all times have experienced. Sensible of this momentous truth, you have improved upon your first essay by the adoption of a Constitution of Government better calculated than your former for an intimate union and for the efficacious management of your common concerns. This Government, the offspring of our own choice, uninfluenced and unawed, adopted upon full investigation and mature deliberation, completely free in its principles, in the distribution of its powers, uniting security with energy, and containing within itself a provision for its own amendment, has a just claim to your confidence and your support. Respect for its authority, compliance with its laws, acquiescence in its measures, are duties enjoined by the fundamental maxims of true liberty. The basis of our political systems is the right of the people to make and to alter their constitutions of government. But the constitution which at any time exists till changed by an explicit and authentic act of the whole people is sacredly obligatory upon all. The very idea of the power and the right of the people to establish government presupposes the duty of every individual to obey the established government.

All obstructions to the execution of the laws, all combinations and associations, under whatever plausible character, with the real design to direct, control, counteract, or awe the regular deliberation and action of the constituted authorities, are destructive of this fundamental principle and of fatal tendency. They serve to organize faction; to give it an artificial and extraordinary force; to put in the place of the delegated will of the nation the will of a party, often a small but artful and enterprising minority of the community, and, according to the alternate triumphs of different parties, to snake the public administration the mirror of the ill-concerted and incongruous projects of faction rather than the organ of consistent and wholesome plans, digested by common counsels and modified by mutual interests.

However combinations or associations of the above description may now and then answer popular ends, they are likely in the course of time and things to become potent engines by which cunning, ambitious, and unprincipled men will be enabled to subvert the power of the people, and to usurp for themselves the reins of government, destroying. afterwards the very engines which have lifted them to unjust dominion.

Toward the preservation of your Government and the permanency of your present happy state, it is requisite not only that you steadily discountenance irregular oppositions to its acknowledged authority, but also that you resist with care the spirit of innovation upon its principles, however specious the pretexts. One method of assault may be to effect in the forms of the Constitution alterations which will impair the energy of the system, and thus to undermine what can not be directly overthrown. In all the changes to which you may be invited remember that time and habit are at least as necessary to fix the true character of governments as of other human institutions; that experience is the surest standard by which to test the real tendency of the existing constitution of a country; that facility in changes upon the credit of mere hypothesis and opinion exposes to perpetual change, from the endless variety of hypothesis and opinion; and remember especially that for the efficient management of your common interests in a country so extensive as ours a government of as much vigor as is consistent with the perfect security of liberty is indispensable. Liberty itself will find in such a government, with powers properly distributed and adjusted, its surest guardian. It is, indeed, little else than a name where the government is too feeble to withstand the enterprises of faction, to confine each member of the society within the limits prescribed by the laws, and to maintain all in the secure and tranquil enjoyment of the rights of person and property.

I have already intimated to you the danger of parties in the State, with particular reference to the founding of them on geographical discriminations. Let me now take a more comprehensive view, and warn you in the most solemn manner against the baneful effects of the spirit of party generally.

This spirit, unfortunately, is inseparable from our nature, having its root in the strongest passions of the human mind. It exists under different shapes in all governments, more or less stifled, controlled, or repressed; but in those of the popular form it is seen in its greatest rankness and is truly their worst enemy.

The alternate domination of one faction over another, sharpened by the spirit of revenge natural to party dissension, which in different ages and countries has perpetrated the most horrid enormities, is itself a frightful despotism. But this leads at length to a more formal and permanent despotism. The disorders and miseries which result gradually incline the minds of men to seek security and repose in the absolute power of an individual, and sooner or later the chief of some prevailing faction, more able or more fortunate than his competitors, turns this disposition to the purposes of his own elevation on the ruins of public liberty.

Without looking forward to an extremity of this kind (which nevertheless ought not to be entirely out of sight), the common and continual mischiefs of the spirit of party are sufficient to make it the interest and duty of a wise people to discourage and restrain it.

It serves always to distract the public councils and enfeeble the public administration. It agitates the community with ill-rounded jealousies and false alarms; kindles the animosity of one part against another; foments occasionally riot and insurrection. It opens the door to foreign influence and corruption, which find a facilitated access to the government itself through the channels of party passion. Thus the policy and the will of one country are subjected to the policy and will of another.

There is an opinion that parties in free countries are useful checks upon the administration of the government, and serve to keep alive the spirit of liberty. This within certain limits is probably true; and in governments of a monarchical cast patriotism may look with indulgence, if not with favor, upon the spirit of party. But in those of the popular character, in governments purely elective, it is a spirit not to be encouraged. From their natural tendency it is certain there will always be enough of that spirit for every salutary purpose; and there being constant danger of excess, the effort ought to be by force of public opinion to mitigate and assuage it. A fire not to be quenched, it demands a uniform vigilance to prevent its bursting into a flame, lest, instead of warming, it should consume.

It is important, likewise, that the habits of thinking in a free country should inspire caution in those intrusted with its administration to confine themselves within their respective constitutional spheres, avoiding in the exercise of the powers of one department to encroach upon another. The spirit of encroachment tends to consolidate the powers of all the departments in one, and thus to create, whatever the form of government, a real despotism. A just estimate of that love of power and proneness to abuse it which predominates in the human heart is sufficient to satisfy us of the truth of this position. The necessity of reciprocal checks in the exercise of political power, by dividing and distributing it into different depositories, and constituting each the guardian of the public weal against invasions by the others, has been evinced by experiments ancient and modern, some of them in our country and under our own eyes. To preserve them must be as necessary as to institute them. If in the opinion of the people the distribution or modification of the constitutional powers be in any particular wrong, let it be corrected by an amendment in the way which the Constitution designates. But let there be no change by usurpation; for though this in one instance may be the instrument of good, it is the customary weapon by which free governments are destroyed. The precedent must always greatly overbalance in permanent evil any partial or transient benefit which the use can at any time yield.

Of all the dispositions and habits which lead to political prosperity, religion and morality are indispensable supports. In vain would that man claim the tribute of patriotism who should labor to subvert these great pillars of human happiness—these firmest props of the duties of men and citizens. The mere politician, equally with the pious man, ought to respect and to cherish them. A volume could not trace all their connections with private and public felicity. Let it simply be asked, Where is the security for property, for reputation, for life, if the sense of religious obligation desert the oaths which are the instruments of investigation in courts of justice? And let us with caution indulge the supposition that morality can be maintained without religion. Whatever may be conceded to the influence of refined education on minds of peculiar structure, reason and experience both forbid us to expect that national morality can prevail in exclusion of religious principle.

It is substantially true that virtue or morality is a necessary spring of popular government. The rule indeed extends with more or less force to every species of free government. Who that is a sincere friend to it can look with indifference upon attempts to shake the foundation of the fabric? Promote, then, as an object of primary importance, institutions 'for the general diffusion of knowledge. In proportion as the structure of a government gives force to public opinion, it is essential that public opinion should be enlightened.

As a very important source of strength and security, cherish public credit. One method of preserving it is to use it as sparingly as possible, avoiding occasions of expense by cultivating peace, but remembering also that timely disbursements to prepare for danger frequently prevent much greater disbursements to repel it; avoiding likewise the accumulation of debt, not only by shunning occasions of expense, but by vigorous exertions in time of peace to discharge the debts which unavoidable wars have occasioned, not ungenerously throwing upon posterity the burthen which we ourselves ought to bear. The execution of these maxims belongs to your representatives; but it is necessary that public opinion should cooperate. To facilitate to them the performance of their duty it is essential that you should practically bear in mind that toward the payment of debts there must be revenue; that to have revenue there must be taxes; that no taxes can be devised which are not more or less inconvenient and unpleasant; that thee intrinsic embarrassment inseparable from the selection of the proper objects (which is always a choice of difficulties), ought to be a decisive motive for a candid construction of the conduct of the Government in making it, and for a spirit of acquiescence in the measures for obtaining revenue which the public exigencies may at any time dictate.

Observe good faith and justice toward all nations. Cultivate peace and harmony with all. Religion and morality enjoin this conduct. And can it be that good policy does not equally enjoin it? It will be worthy of a free, enlightened, and at no distant period a great nation to give to mankind the magnanimous and too novel example of a people always guided by an exalted justice and benevolence. Who can doubt that in the course of time and things the fruits of such a plan would richly repay any temporary advantages which might be lost by a steady adherence to it? Can it be that Providence has not connected the permanent felicity of a nation with its virtue? The experiment, at least, is recommended by every sentiment which ennobles human nature. Alas! is it rendered impossible by its vices?

In the execution of such a plan nothing is more essential than that permanent, inveterate antipathies against particular nations and passionate attachments for others should be excluded, and that in place of them just and amicable feelings toward all should be cultivated. The nation which indulges toward another an habitual hatred or an habitual fondness is in some degree a slave. It is a slave to its animosity or to its affection, either of which is sufficient to lead it astray from its duty and its interest. Antipathy in one nation against another disposes each more readily to offer insult and injury, to lay hold of slight causes of umbrage, and to be haughty and intractable when accidental or trifling occasions of dispute occur.

Hence frequent collisions, obstinate, envenomed, and bloody contests. The nation prompted by ill will and resentment sometimes impels to war the government contrary to the best calculations of policy. The government sometimes participates in the national propensity, and adopts through passion what reason would reject. At other times it makes the animosity of the nation subservient to projects of hostility, instigated by pride, ambition, and other sinister and pernicious motives. The peace often, sometimes perhaps the liberty, of nations has been the victim.

So, likewise, a passionate attachment of one nation for another produces a variety of evils. Sympathy for the favorite nation, facilitating the illusion of an imaginary common interest in cases where no real common interest exists, and infusing into one the enmities of the other, betrays the former into a participation in the quarrels and wars of the latter without adequate inducement or justification. It leads also to concessions to the favorite nation of privileges denied to others, which is apt doubly to injure the nation making the concessions by unnecessarily parting with what ought to have been retained, and by exciting jealousy, ill will, and a disposition to retaliate in the parties from whom equal privileges are withheld; and it gives to ambitions, corrupted, or deluded citizens (who devote themselves to the favorite nation) facility to betray or sacrifice the interests of their own country without odium, sometimes even with popularity, gilding with the appearances of a virtuous sense of obligation, a commendable deference for public opinion, or a laudable zeal for public good the base or foolish compliances of ambition, corruption, or infatuation.

As avenues to foreign influence in innumerable ways, such attachments are particularly alarming to the truly enlightened and independent patriot. How many opportunities do they afford to tamper with domestic factions, to practice the arts of seduction, to mislead public opinion, to influence or awe the public councils! Such an attachment of a small or weak toward a great and powerful nation dooms the former to be the satellite of the latter. Against the insidious wiles of foreign influence (I conjure you to believe me, fellow-citizens) the jealousy of a free people ought to be constantly awake, since history and experience prove that foreign influence is one of the most baneful foes of republican government. But that jealousy, to be useful, must be impartial, else it becomes the instrument of the very influence to be avoided, instead of a defense against it. Excessive partiality for one foreign nation and excessive dislike of another cause those whom they actuate to see danger only on one side, and serve to veil and even second the arts of influence on the other. Real patriots who may resist the intrigues of the favorite are liable to become suspected and odious, while its tools and dupes usurp the applause and confidence of the people to surrender their interests.

The great rule of conduct for us in regard to foreign nations is, in extending our commercial relations to have with them as little political connection as possible. So far as we have already formed engagements let them be fulfilled with perfect good faith. Here let us stop.

Europe has a set of primary interests which to us have none or a very remote relation. Hence she must be engaged in frequent controversies, the causes of which are essentially foreign to our concerns. Hence, therefore, it must be unwise in us to implicate ourselves by artificial ties in the ordinary vicissitudes of her politics or the ordinary combinations and collisions of her friendships or enmities.

Our detached and distant situation invites and enables us to pursue a different course. If we remain one people, under an efficient government, the period is not far off when we may defy material injury from external annoyance; when we may take such an attitude as will cause the neutrality we may at any time resolve upon to be scrupulously respected; when belligerent nations, under the impossibility of making acquisitions upon us, will not lightly hazard the giving us provocation; when we may choose peace or war, as our interest, guided by justice, shall counsel.

Why forego the advantages of so peculiar a situation? Why quit our own to stand upon foreign ground? Why, by interweaving our destiny with that of any part of Europe, entangle our peace and prosperity in the toils of European ambition, rivalship, interest, humor, or caprice?

It is our true policy to steer clear of permanent alliances with any portion of the foreign world, so far, I mean, as we are now at liberty to do it; for let me not be understood as capable of patronizing infidelity to existing engagements. I hold the maxim no less applicable to public than to private affairs that honesty is always. The best policy. I repeat, therefore, let those engagements be unwise to extend them.

Taking care always to keep ourselves by suitable establishments on a respectable defensive posture, we may safely trust to temporary alliances for extraordinary emergencies.

Harmony, liberal intercourse with all nations are recommended by policy, humanity, and interest. But even our commercial policy should hold an equal and impartial hand, neither seeking nor granting exclusive favors or preferences; consulting the natural course of things; diffusing and diversifying by gentle means the streams of commerce, but forcing nothing; establishing with powers so disposed, in order to give trade a stable course, to define the rights of our merchants, and to enable the Government to support them, conventional rules of intercourse, the best that present circumstances and mutual opinion will permit, but temporary and liable to be from time to time abandoned or varied as experience and circumstances shall dictate; constantly keeping in view that it is folly in one nation to look for disinterested favors from another; that it must pay with a portion of its independence for whatever it may accept under that character; that by such acceptance it may place itself in the condition of having given equivalents for nominal favors, and yet of being reproached with ingratitude for not giving more. There can be no greater error than to expect or calculate upon real favors from nation to nation. It is an illusion which experience must cure, which a just pride ought to discard.

In offering to you, my countrymen, these counsels of an old and affectionate friend I dare not hope they will make the strong and lasting impression I could wish—that they will control the usual current of the passions or prevent our nation from running the course which has hitherto marked the destiny of nations. But if I may even flatter myself that they may be productive of some partial benefit, some occasional good—that they may now and then recur to moderate the fury of party spirit, to warn against the mischiefs of foreign intrigue, to guard against the impostures of pretended patriotism— this hope will be a full recompense for the solicitude for your welfare by which they have been dictated.

How far in the discharge of my official duties I have been guided by the principles which have been delineated the public records and other evidences of my conduct must witness to you and to the world. To myself, the assurance of my own conscience is that I have at least believed myself to be guided by them.

In relation to the still subsisting war in Europe my proclamation of the 22d of April, 1793, is the index to my plan. Sanctioned by your approving voice and by that of your representatives in both Houses of Congress, the spirit of that measure has continually governed me, uninfluenced by any attempts to deter or divert me from it.

After deliberate examination, with the aid of the best lights I could obtain, I was well satisfied that our country, under all the circumstances of the case, had a right to take, and was bound in duty and interest to take, a neutral position. Having taken it, I determined as far as should depend upon me to maintain it with moderation, perseverance, and firmness.

The considerations which respect the right to hold this conduct it is not necessary on this occasion to detail. I will only observe that, according to my understanding of the matter, that right, so far from being denied by any of the belligerent powers, has been virtually admitted by all.

The duty of holding a neutral conduct may be inferred, without anything more, from the obligation which justice and humanity impose on every nation, in cases in which it is free to act, to maintain inviolate the relations of peace and amity toward other nations.

The inducements of interest for observing that conduct will best be referred to your own reflections and experience. With me a predominant motive has been to endeavor to gain time to our country to settle and mature its yet recent institutions, and to progress without interruption to that degree of strength and consistency which is necessary to give it, humanly speaking, the command of its own fortunes.

Though in reviewing the incidents of my Administration I am unconscious of intentional error, I am nevertheless too sensible of my defects not to think it probable that I may have committed many errors. Whatever they may be, I fervently beseech the Almighty to avert or mitigate the evils to which they may tend. I shall also carry with me the hope that my country will never cease to view them with indulgence, and that, after forty-five years of my life dedicated to its service with an upright zeal, the faults of incompetent abilities will be consigned to oblivion, as myself must soon be to the mansions of rest.

Relying on its kindness in this as in other things, and actuated by that fervent love toward it which is so natural to a man who views in it the native soil of himself and his progenitors for several generations, I anticipate with pleasing expectation that retreat in which I promise myself to realize without alloy the sweet enjoyment of partaking in the midst of my fellow-citizens the benign influence of good laws under a free government—the ever-favorite object of my heart, and the happy reward, as I trust, of our mutual cares, labors, and dangers.

ALSO AVAILABLE

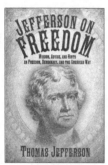

$ 9.95 Hardcover
978-1-61608-289-5

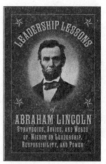

$ 9.95 Hardcover
978-1-61608-412-7

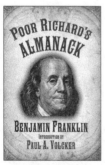

$ 9.95 Hardcover
978-1-60239-117-8

$ 9.95 Hardcover
978-1-61608-351-9